WARS THAT CHANGED AMERICAN HISTORY

The Civil War

Deborah DeFord

WORLD ALMANAC® LIBRARY

Please visit our Web site at: www.garethstevens.com
For a free color catalog describing World Almanac® Library's list of high-quality books
and multimedia programs, call 1-800-848-2928 (USA) or 1-800-387-3178 (Canada).
World Almanac® Library's fax: (414) 332-3567

Library of Congress Catalog-in-Publication Data

DeFord, Deborah H.
    The Civil War / by Deborah DeFord. — North American ed.
        p. cm. — (Wars that changed American history)
    Includes bibliographical references and index.
    ISBN-10: 0-8368-7291-6 – ISBN-13: 978-0-8368-7291-0 (lib. bdg.)
    ISBN-10: 0-8368-7300-9 – ISBN-13: 978-0-8368-7300-9 (softcover)
    1. United States—History—Civil War, 1861-1865—Juvenile literature.
    I. Title.   II. Series.
    E468.D425   2007
    973.7—dc22   2006011601

First published in 2007 by
World Almanac® Library
A Member of the WRC Media Family of Companies
330 West Olive Street, Suite 100
Milwaukee, WI 53212 USA

A Creative Media Applications, Inc. Production
Design and Production: Alan Barnett, Inc.
Editor: Susan Madoff
Copy Editor: Laurie Lieb
Proofreader: Laurie Lieb and Donna Drybread
Indexer: Nara Wood
World Almanac® Library editorial direction: Mark J. Sachner
World Almanac® Library editor: Alan Wachtel
World Almanac® Library art direction: Tammy West
World Almanac® Library production: Jessica Morris

Picture credits: New York Public Library, Astor, Lenox and Tilden Foundations: pages 5, 6, 16, 23, 24, 38; Library of
Congress: pages 10, 12, 20, 26, 29, 31, 33, 34, 41; Associated Press: pages 13, 15, 25, 32, 36; Picture History: page 21;
The Granger Collection: page 22, 43; Maps courtesy of Ortelius Design

Printed in the United States of America

1 2 3 4 5 6 7 8 9 10 09 08 07 06

Table of Contents

Cover: A painting illustrating the Civil War Battle of Pea Ridge, fought in Arkansas on March 7–8, 1862. The battle ended in a victory for the Union forces led by General Samuel R. Curtis. Approximately 1,400 Union soldiers died on the battlefield, while Confederate forces lost 4,600 men.

From the time when America declared its independence in the 1700s to the present, every war in which Americans have fought has been a turning point in the nation's history. All of the major wars of American history have been bloody, and all of them have brought tragic loss of life. Some of them have been credited with great results, while others partly or entirely failed to achieve their goals. Some of them were widely supported; others were controversial and exposed deep divisions within the American people. None will ever be forgotten.

The American Revolution created a new type of nation based on the idea that the government should serve the people. As a result of the Mexican-American War, the young country expanded dramatically. Controversy over slavery in the new territory stoked the broader controversy between Northern and Southern states over the slavery issue and powers of state governments versus the federal government. When the slave states seceded, President Abraham Lincoln led the Union into a war against the Confederacy—the Civil War—that reunited a divided nation and ended slavery.

▼ Wars have shaped the history of the United States of America since the nation was founded in 1776. Conflict in this millennium continues to alter the decisions the government makes and the role the United States plays on the world stage.

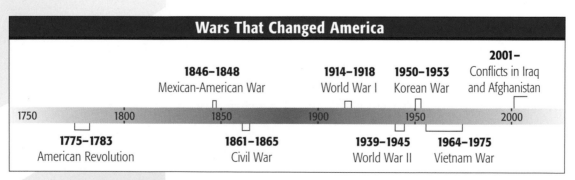

Wars That Changed America

	1846–1848 Mexican-American War	**1914–1918** World War I	**1950–1953** Korean War	**2001–** Conflicts in Iraq and Afghanistan
1750 — 1800 — 1850 — 1900 — 1950 — 2000				
1775–1783 American Revolution	**1861–1865** Civil War	**1939–1945** World War II	**1964–1975** Vietnam War	

The roles that the United States played in World War I and World War II helped transform the country into a major world power. In both these wars, the entry of the United States helped turn the tide of the war.

Later in the twentieth century, the United States engaged in a Cold War rivalry with the Soviet Union. During this time, the United States fought two wars to prevent the spread of communism. The Korean War essentially ended in a stalemate, and after years of combat in the Vietnam War, the United States withdrew. Both claimed great numbers of American lives, and following its defeat in Vietnam, the United States became more cautious in its use of military force.

That trend changed when the United States led the war that drove invading Iraqi forces from Kuwait in 1990. After the al-Qaeda terrorist attacks of September 11, 2001, the United States again led a war, this time against Afghanistan, which was sheltering al-Qaeda. About two years later, the United States led the invasion that toppled Iraq's dictatorship.

In this book, readers will learn about the complex issues facing the United States in 1861 which led to the Civil War. Brought together and bound by common elements, the United States of America faced its greatest challenge since independence when citizens were forced to pick up arms against each other in a struggle that pitted one way of life against another. President Abraham Lincoln saw only one option— unity—and the Union victory in the war set the stage for the way the nation would go forward to this day.

▲ *The Union ironclad* Monitor *and Confederate* Virginia *(formerly the* Merrimack*) face off in the famous "Battle of the Ironclads" in March 1862. The battle ended in a stalemate but signaled a great change in sea fighting. The two ships dueled for five hours and were so close that they collided five times.*

CHAPTER 1

One Nation or Two?

▼ *Slaves work on a cotton **plantation** in the Old South in 1859. The Southern economy relied on slaves to perform the backbreaking work of harvesting cotton in the stifling heat and humidity.*

In 1850, the United States was still a young country. The American people had many disagreements about how the national government and the state governments should work together. Many people believed strongly that each state had ultimate power over how it would be run and what relationship it would have with the Union as a whole. Others held that the federal (national) government bound the states into one united nation with certain laws in common, based on the Constitution, and other laws left up to individual state governments. Before the Civil War, people generally referred to "these United States" in the plural. After the war, people would speak of "the United States" as one single nation-state.

Before the war, disagreement over the relationship of the federal and state governments grew especially intense concerning the issue of slavery. Slavery had existed in North America from the early days of European colonization. In the Southern states of what became the United States, people came to depend on slave labor to make cash crops such as tobacco, rice, **indigo**, sugar, and cotton highly profitable.

Over the years since settlement, however, people in Europe and the Americas had increasingly questioned whether it was morally acceptable to enslave a person. Following the example of other nations, the United States banned the importation of black slaves in 1804. In the North, one state after another planned for the eventual **abolition** of slavery and made it illegal to buy new slaves. The leaders of the South had no intention of doing the same. By 1819, the states were equally divided into two sections: "free" states (where slavery was not allowed) and "slave" states (where slavery was legal).

This conflict became more important as new territories west of the Mississippi River opened up for settlement. Southern planters saw vast lands that could be planted with cash crops, with the help of slave labor. Many Northerners, however, did not want slavery to spread. The dispute raised a frightening question. Would the Union be strong enough to hold the states together as a single nation? The Civil War would answer the question and finally abolish slavery—throughout the country—for good.

The Missouri Compromise of 1820

In the decades leading up to the war, leaders in the federal government decided that the best way to settle the fight over the spread of slavery was to come up with a **compromise**. The Missouri Compromise of 1820 allowed Missouri to enter the Union as a slave state at the same time that Maine entered as a free state, maintaining the balance of free and slave states. The Missouri Compromise also drew a line across the existing unorganized U.S. **territories** at the latitude of 36°30'. Above that line, with the

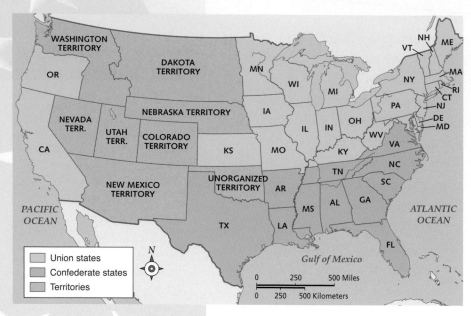

In this map, the states that remained loyal to the Union are shown in yellow. Those that seceded and formed the Confederate States of America are shown in green. A portion of western Virginia seceded from Virginia and was admitted to the Union in 1863 as West Virginia. The four "Border States" that permitted slavery but did not favor **secession** were Delaware, Maryland, Kentucky, and Missouri.

exception of Missouri, slavery was prohibited.

By 1850, the nation included fifteen free and fifteen slave states. Southerners continued to worry that slave states would soon be outnumbered. In part, their concern arose from the effect of slaveholding on their power in Congress.

Because of its large plantations run on slave labor, the South had fewer cities and much smaller populations than the North, which limited the number of votes the Southern states were allowed in the House of **Representatives**. In addition, Southern states got less than one representative vote for each slave. They needed at least as many slave states in the Union as free states if they wanted to maintain a strong voice in the federal government. When antislavery forces in Congress tried to prohibit slavery in territory won in the Mexican-American War (1846–1848), Southern legislators decided they would have to take steps to safeguard the institution of slavery. If they could not maintain slavery in the South, they decided they would leave the Union (secede).

The Compromise of 1850

In the Compromise of 1850, Congress intended to settle the slavery issue once and for all. After many months of **debate**, the members of Congress accepted the Compromise in September. The Compromise

The Civil War

admitted California as a free state, which pleased people opposed to the spread of slavery. In addition, it created New Mexico and Utah without restriction on slavery, which meant that voters in these states could choose for themselves whether to allow slavery. This pleased those in favor of allowing slavery's spread. Finally, the Compromise established the Texas border and ended the slave trade (but not slavery) in the District of Columbia.

The Compromise also enacted the Fugitive Slave Act, a law stating that runaway slaves must be returned to their owners, even if they had escaped into "free" territory years earlier. The act further stated that bystanders must assist slave catchers. Anyone who hid a slave or helped one escape would be fined and imprisoned. According to the act, escaped slaves had no right to a trial by jury or testimony in their own defense. This act was perhaps the most troubling part of the entire Compromise for abolitionists.

Rips in the Seams of the Nation

The Fugitive Slave Act brought the ugliness of slavery into clear view for many in the North. The sight of African Americans being forcibly captured and carried away made a deep impression. Abolitionists strengthened their pleas for the end of slavery. In 1852, for example, the success of Harriet Beecher Stowe's novel *Uncle Tom's Cabin* caused many people to finally take a stand against the perpetuation and spread of slavery.

Meanwhile, a railroad was proposed that would run west to the Pacific Ocean. Senator Stephen A. Douglas believed that the new railroad would encourage expansion westward and new prosperity for the nation, but he knew that the ongoing conflict over the spread of slavery could slow development. He

"The Book That Made This Great War"

Harriet Beecher Stowe (1811–1896) grew up in a family deeply opposed to slavery. When the Fugitive Slave Act (1850) brought slave catchers into the Northern states to capture former slaves, Stowe's dismay about slavery boiled over. Stowe drew on memories of the time she had lived in Ohio, a free state just across the Ohio River from the slave state Kentucky, to write a novel describing the horrors of slavery. First published as a series in a weekly antislavery newspaper called the *National Era, Uncle Tom's Cabin* was published as a book in 1852. It immediately sold 300,000 copies, and within ten years, it sold two million copies.

Stowe's characters and descriptions in *Uncle Tom's Cabin* convinced many Northerners that slavery must end and convinced Southern slaveholders that the North wanted to destroy their way of life. Years later, with the Civil War raging, the story circulated that President Abraham Lincoln, on meeting Stowe, greeted her as the woman who wrote "the book that made this great war."

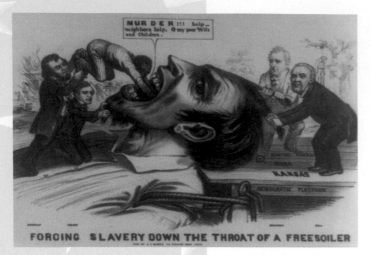

FORCING SLAVERY DOWN THE THROAT OF A FREESOILER

▲ *A political cartoon drawn in 1856 blames the Democratic Party for the violence over slavery in Kansas. A bearded "free-soiler" (a member of a political party opposing the extension of slavery into the territories and opposing slavery itself) is strapped down and restrained by two small figures, known to be Democrats. Democratic senator Stephen A. Douglas (right) and President Franklin Pierce (left) force a black man into the free-soiler's mouth as he screams for help, illustrating the title of the cartoon, "Forcing Slavery Down the Throat of a Freesoiler." The platform the head is resting on is marked Kansas, Cuba, and Central America, indicating the ambition of Democrats to extend slavery into these areas.*

therefore proposed the Kansas-Nebraska Act. The act created a Kansas Territory and a Nebraska Territory. It also provided that the dividing line between slave and free states established by the Missouri Compromise would be completely replaced by the provisions of the Compromise of 1850 that allowed voters in a new territory to decide whether to allow slavery or not. In 1854, Congress passed the Kansas-Nebraska Act. People on both sides of the issue rushed to Kansas. Antislavery forces raised money to arm **"free-soil"** settlers and send them into the region. Armed proslavery men from throughout the South, and especially from Kansas's neighbor Missouri, raced to the region as well. Violence erupted on the contested soil, and the region soon became known as "Bleeding Kansas."

One militant abolitionist living in Kansas was John Brown. He decided to "fight fire with fire," he told his son, and "strike terror in the hearts of the proslavery people." On May 24, 1856, he led a small group carrying sharpened broadswords into a proslavery settlement at Pottawatomie Creek, Kansas. The abolitionists kidnapped and murdered five men. Brown and others went on to form violent bands of armed men who roamed the countryside, terrorizing the proslavery settlers.

The 1860 Election Approaches

The slavery issue would not die. In March 1857, the Supreme Court decided a case concerning a slave named Dred Scott. Scott's owner had taken him from Missouri to live for a number of years in the

The Civil War

Wisconsin Territory, a region that was free according to the Missouri Compromise. After they returned to Missouri, the slaveholder died. Scott's new owner moved from Missouri to New York, leaving Scott behind. Based on his years living in a free territory, Scott went to court to sue for his freedom.

The Supreme Court decided that Scott, as a slave, did not have a **citizen**'s right to sue in a federal court. The Court also declared that no African American, whether slave or free, could be a U.S. citizen and that Congress had no constitutional right to declare Wisconsin a free or slave territory. With that decision, the Supreme Court undid the Missouri Compromise (in which Congress had specifically declared certain regions "slave" or "free") once and for all. The Court's decision also nullified the Compromise of 1850, in which California had entered the Union as a free state. While the decision did not specifically mention the Western territories that the Compromise of 1850 had covered, it was assumed that the decision applied to California (in addition to any individual state where slavery was prohibited).

Once again, abolitionists and other opponents of slavery raised a cry. It seemed clear to some people that the controversy over slavery must finally be settled or the nation was lost. The writer Ralph Waldo Emerson declared, "I do not see how a barbarous community and a civilized community can constitute one state. I think we must get rid of slavery, or we must get rid of freedom."

Meanwhile, John Brown, who traveled in disguise to avoid capture and punishment for the murders in Kansas, decided it was time to strike another blow for his cause. He gathered a band of followers to capture the federal **arsenal** in Harpers Ferry, Virginia. Once they had access to guns and ammunition, they

Debating the Future of the United States

In 1858, two men sought election to Illinois's seat for the U.S. Senate. Stephen A. Douglas was the incumbent senator and a Democrat. Opposing him was a Republican lawyer named Abraham Lincoln. Lincoln challenged Douglas to a series of seven debates to be held throughout Illinois. In one of the debates Lincoln argued that the states must come to a united agreement on the future of slavery. "A house divided against itself cannot stand," he declared. Douglas asked, "Are you in favor of conferring upon the negro the rights and privileges of citizenship?" Lincoln replied, "I am not, nor ever have been in favor of bringing about in any way the social and political equality of the white and black races. There must be the position of superior and inferior." He went on, however, to say that African Americans were entitled to "life, liberty, and the pursuit of happiness."

Douglas won the senate seat. Lincoln, however, won national respect among Republicans. In 1860, he won the presidential election.

planned to arm all the slaves of the region and stage a massive rebellion against the slaveholders.

Brown and his followers in the armory were quickly surrounded and arrested. In response to

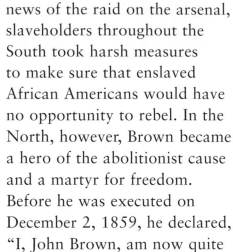

news of the raid on the arsenal, slaveholders throughout the South took harsh measures to make sure that enslaved African Americans would have no opportunity to rebel. In the North, however, Brown became a hero of the abolitionist cause and a martyr for freedom. Before he was executed on December 2, 1859, he declared, "I, John Brown, am now quite certain that the crimes of this guilty land will never be purged away but with Blood."

▲ *An 1861 sketch shows John Brown, the abolitionist, and some of his followers arrested and injured after law enforcement officials stopped their attack on the federal arsenal at Harpers Ferry, Virginia. Brown had planned to steal weapons from the arsenal to arm slaves in the region.*

Mr. President, Abraham Lincoln

Brown's raid stirred abolitionist fervor and may very well have inched Abraham Lincoln just far enough ahead for victory in the presidential election of 1860. Lincoln, portrayed by the Republican Party as "Honest Old Abe," won the election with less than 40 percent of the popular vote, although his electoral support in the North was solid. Ten Southern states never even put his name on the **ballot.**

The Republicans now held the chief office of the United States. They failed, however, to gain a majority in either house of Congress. In the North, abolitionists rejoiced to have a president who seemed sympathetic to their cause. In the South, political leaders saw only catastrophe. For some, the question whether the United States could stand in the face of its divisions was finally answered, and the answer was no.

The Civil War

CHAPTER 2

To War

Lincoln won the presidential election in 1860 with the promise of a railroad that would span the continent and a **homesteading** law that would help Americans settle the vast open spaces of the West. On the subject of slavery, however, he was more cautious, despite the words that appeared on Republican campaign coins (handed out like modern-day political buttons): "Millions for freedom; not one cent for slavery." Lincoln made clear that his primary concern was not slavery, but keeping the Union together.

In the South, leaders were convinced otherwise. One after another equated Lincoln's election with the cause of Northern abolitionists. After Lincoln's election, South Carolina congressman Lawrence M. Keitt

▼ In 1862, well-known Civil War photographer Alexander Gardner captured President Lincoln, General George B. McClellan, and his staff in camp at Antietam, Maryland, the site of a pivotal battle during the Civil War.

wrote, "How can we stand it?... It is enough to risk disunion for." A speech delivered by U.S. senator Robert Toombs in Alabama bore the title, "The Election of Lincoln Is Sufficient Cause for Secession." An editor for the *Southern Confederacy*, a Georgia newspaper, declared, "the South will never submit to such humiliation and degradation as the **inauguration** of Abraham Lincoln."

With Lincoln's election, the Southern states moved quickly to leave the Union. South Carolina led the way with a convention to debate secession. Marching bands played, fireworks exploded in the sky, citizens waved state flags, and the state **militia** marched. On December 20, 1860, after a vote of 169 to zero, South Carolina dissolved all ties to the United States. Other Southern states quickly followed: Mississippi (January 9, 1861), Florida (January 10), Alabama (January 11), Georgia (January 19), Louisiana (January 26), and Texas (February 1).

The Beginning of Armed Conflict

The states that seceded were led by people who believed that their action was legal. They believed that a state's government had authority above that of the federal government. As soon as these states broke free of the Union, they set up a new federal government of their own, which they called the Confederate States of America (CSA).

Delegates from the seceded states elected the U.S. senator from Mississippi, Jefferson Davis, as their new president. After locating their capital in Richmond, Virginia, the new Confederate leaders began to take possession of federal property, such as forts, customhouses (responsible for collecting import taxes), and arsenals.

Meanwhile, during the four months between Lincoln's election in November and his inauguration in March, President James Buchanan continued in office. He refused to accept the Southern states' right to secede, but he also refused to use force to keep them from taking control of federal property. In January 1861, he declared to Congress that the Union was "a sacred trust." He held the continued responsibility, he said, to collect revenues (taxes) and protect government property in the seceded states. Yet he did not take any action.

Among the property Southerners intended to seize was Fort Sumter, under the command of Major Robert Anderson, in Charleston, South Carolina. It was one of just a few government properties in the South still under the control of the Union. Buchanan sent an unarmed ship to the fort with needed food. Before the supplies could be landed, the South Carolina militia fired on the ship and forced it to leave.

When Lincoln entered his presidential office for the first time after his inauguration, he found a message from Major Anderson. Supplies for the men at Fort Sumter were dwindling, Anderson reported. They had enough for no more than six weeks, and South Carolina's governor, Francis W. Pickens, was demanding their immediate surrender.

Lincoln made the momentous decision to maintain the fort as a federal post, despite the governor's demands. Lincoln planned to send a **fleet** of warships to anchor outside Charleston's harbor. Smaller boats would then secretly carry troops and supplies to Sumter under cover of dark in order to prevent the South Carolina militia from interfering. The warships would protect these other boats and divert the militia's attention from the secret activity. He gave his order on April 4, 1861. Jefferson Davis

Lincoln's First Inaugural Address

Lincoln, pictured here, during his inauguration as the sixteenth president of the United States on March 4, 1861, on the steps of the half-finished Capitol Building in Washington, D.C. To encourage the Confederate states to return to the Union, Lincoln promised that he would not interfere with slavery where it already existed. He would enforce the Fugitive Slave Act. On the other hand, he stated that he was willing to use the force necessary to hold the Union together.

Most important, Lincoln pleaded for unity. "We are not enemies, but friends," he declared. "The mystic chords of memory, stretching from every battlefield, and patriot grave, to every living heart and hearthstone, all over this broad land, will yet swell the chorus of the Union, when again touched, as surely they will be, by the better angels of our nature."

▼ Union monitors (iron-clads) fire upon Fort Sumter on Sullivan's Island, located in the harbor at Charleston, South Carolina, on April 7, 1863. The large fleet, which had sailed to the region a month earlier, included the massive ship The New Ironsides *and the double-turret tinclad* Keokuk. *These vessels were able to get close to their target on shore due to their iron protection. Other ships in the illustration are the* Weehawken, Montauk, Passaic, Catskill, Nahant, Patapsco, *and* Nantucket. *The* Weehawken *grounded in the harbor and received heavy gunfire from the Confederate fort, as did the* Keokuk, *which sank the following day.*

responded with orders to his commander in Charleston, General Pierre G. T. Beauregard, to resist. As the Union fleet approached on April 12, South Carolina troops opened fire that continued for forty hours. The Union fleet was prevented from completing its delivery to Fort Sumter. When Major Anderson ran out of supplies on April 13, he was forced to surrender the fort to the Confederacy.

The War Is On

The fall of Fort Sumter created a landslide of patriotism in both the North and the South. With only sixteen thousand men in the U.S. fighting forces, Lincoln requested that seventy-five thousand state militia troops be released for national duty to help put down the rebellion. Northern governors offered twice that number. In the South, on the other hand, people accused Lincoln of launching an "unholy crusade" against what they considered their basic right to govern themselves. Four more slave states decided to leave the Union. Conventions gathered and voted in favor of secession in Virginia (April 17), Arkansas (May 6), North Carolina (May 20), and Tennessee (June 8).

Throughout the South, a significant minority still wanted to save the Union. Most Southerners, however, continued to claim that each state should be allowed to make its own laws without federal interference. The Southern Democrats' understanding of what the Constitution said on the

The Civil War

subject was different from Lincoln's. They especially stood firm on what they regarded as their constitutional right to decide the question of slavery. When President Davis called for more troops, recruits arrived not only from the states that had seceded, but also from Maryland, Missouri, Kentucky, and the Oklahoma Indian territory. Although these places remained officially part of the Union, many individuals there were proslavery and agreed with the Confederate position on states' rights.

As both sides of the conflict geared up for war, the North had an important advantage over the South. It had far more developed industries, while the South depended on agriculture for most of its wealth. War required not only fighting men, but also weapons and ammunition, uniforms and boots, and means of transporting large numbers of people and supplies to the battle zones. Both sides were seriously short of weapons and would continue to be throughout the war. Even so, the North kept its advantage.

More than 90 percent of the nation's firearms were produced in the North. The same was true of locomotives to pull trains, footwear, **pig iron** for ammunition, and cloth for uniforms. In addition, the North had double the mileage of railroad tracks as the South and an even greater percentage of canals and paved roadways.

The one advantage the South had was its food production. It lacked adequate railroad lines, however, and it was plagued by enemy troops in the region. Southern leaders found it hard to move the food and supplies to where Confederate troops needed them most. For war supplies of all kinds, the South would need to trade cotton with England. Because this trade required open seaways for shipping, it opened yet another weakness that the North would soon exploit.

War and Technology

In many ways, the Civil War was the first modern war fought by the United States. Transportation was undergoing a revolution with the arrival of train lines that would soon span the continent. Steam locomotives carried soldiers and supplies to battle. Ironclad ships fought at sea.

The electric **telegraph**, invented by Samuel Morse in 1844, allowed military leaders and news correspondents to communicate instantly over vast distances. The Union government seized control of existing telegraph service, and its military added more than 15,000 miles (24,000 kilometers) of line during the war.

At the same time, a new wet-plate process in photography made it possible for photographers to take pictures on fields of battle, showing ordinary civilians the horrors of war.

Technology had its limits. Railroad tracks could be torn up; telegraph wires could be cut; photographers sometimes staged their photos. Yet the technologies radically changed how news, people, and supplies traveled, helping to change, in turn, people's views about the war.

▼ *This map of the major battles of the Civil War illustrates the Union blockade, which lasted for the first two years of the war, in addition to the direction of General Sherman's March to the Sea. Union victories are marked in blue, Confederate victories are marked in black, and the states' affiliations in yellow, orange, and green.*

N o one in either the North or the South expected the Civil War to turn into the major war it became. The young nation, however, had never worked out the details of the balance of power between the federal government and state governments. Now, the North fought to stop the Southern states from leaving the Union. The Union could not be dissolved, Unionists such as Lincoln declared; they believed the future of the country depended on unity.

In contrast, the secessionists were convinced that each state was sovereign (its own boss). They

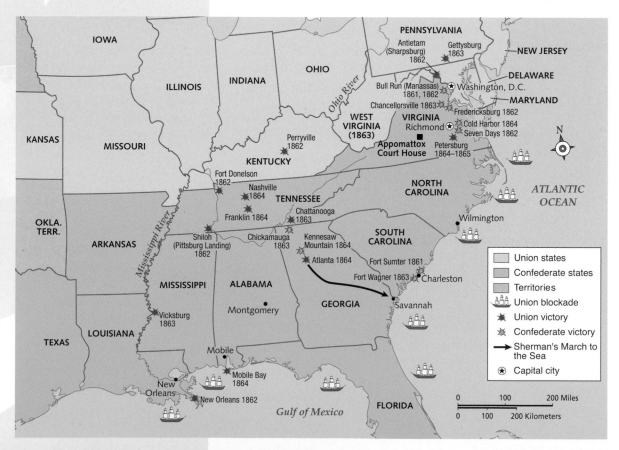

believed when the federal government tried to meddle in the decisions that belonged to a state, that state had the right to reject the federal government.

The Border States

Four slave states, all in the Upper South, did not secede. These states, Delaware, Kentucky, Missouri, and Maryland, became known as the Border States. (Later, in 1863, the western part of Virginia would break off from the rest of the state to become a pro-Union Border State called West Virginia.) Delaware quickly joined the Union effort outright. Kentucky, whose citizens were divided on the issue, remained neutral and officially sent no troops to either side.

Missouri was hopelessly divided, with skirmishing civilians of Union and Confederate factions carrying on the violence that had made neighboring Kansas an ongoing battleground. Maryland, which bordered Washington, D.C., was also divided. The potential danger in this split appeared even before Lincoln's election, when a plot to **assassinate** him as he changed trains in Baltimore, Maryland, was uncovered. Later, on April 19, 1861, the Sixth Massachusetts regiment marched through Baltimore on its way to Washington. Violence erupted, and four soldiers and a dozen Baltimore citizens died. Lincoln declared martial law in the region. Soon after, the state legislature declared neutrality for Maryland. Then it took steps to affirm the state's loyalty to the Union.

The First Major Battle on Land

While the states chose their sides and the two governments hurried to gather enough troops and **armaments**, Lincoln and his advisers decided how to direct a war against the Confederacy. When news spread that the

Fast Fact

Confederate army general Thomas Jackson received the nickname he became known by, "Stonewall" Jackson, because he and his troops stood like a stone wall against Union troops at the First Battle of Bull Run at Manassas Junction in 1861.

Confederate capital had been moved to Richmond, close to the Union capital in Washington, D.C., Northerners demanded that the North invade the South. The Confederate Congress was scheduled to meet in Richmond on July 20, 1861. In response, headlines in the *New York Tribune* read, "Forward to Richmond! The Richmond Congress Must Not Be Allowed to Meet There."

Against the advice of experienced military leaders, Lincoln sent General Irvin McDowell with about thirty-five thousand brand-new soldiers to march on Manassas Junction (Bull Run), Virginia, where twenty thousand Confederate troops had gathered to guard a railroad depot. Lincoln feared that the depot would provide a vital link for Southern troops if the Confederate leaders decided to send troops north to attack Washington. One writer for the Washington *Star* wrote of the Union troops: "regiment after regiment was seen...their arms gleaming in the sun.... Cheer after cheer was heard as regiment greeted regiment, and this with the martial music and sharp clear orders of commanding officers."

Hundreds of Washington reporters, civilians, and Congress members followed McDowell's army to Manassas Junction, expecting to watch a victorious battle against the South. They brought picnic meals, champagne, and binoculars, eager to see the Union soldiers "thrash the Rebs [rebels]."

At first, the battle looked as if it would give the Union a major victory. Then the tide turned, as eleven thousand newly arrived Confederate reinforcements took the Union soldiers by surprise. Northern civilians watching from 2 miles (3.2 km) away saw more smoke than fighting, but they were close enough to see untrained Union soldiers who panicked and ran away. According to one congressman, "No mortal ever saw such a mass of ghastly wretches. The further they ran, the more frightened they grew."

Before the day ended, 625 Union soldiers were dead, 950 wounded, and 1,200 captured. On the Confederate side, 400 had died and 1,600 were wounded. The battle was the first of numerous humiliating defeats for the North throughout the first two years of the war.

▲ *Confederate soldiers pose for a picture in Richmond, Virginia, before they leave to battle Union troops.*

Unexpected Soldiers

Not all the soldiers and officers in the armies were men. It is now known that hundreds of women disguised themselves as men so they could take up arms and fight. Other women served as spies, although many of them were captured and imprisoned until the war ended.

Children, too, joined the army. They were not allowed to enlist as fighters, but some became the youngest members of the regimental bands or the fife-and-drum corps. The bands played for parades, formations, and concerts. The drummers woke the soldiers in the morning and signaled "lights out" at night. They communicated the commanders' orders to troops on the battlefield as well. Buglers most often accompanied the horse-riding cavalry.

The War at Sea

The Union's military goal was first to cut the Confederacy off from its sources of war supplies from Europe. On April 19, 1861, Lincoln proclaimed a **blockade** against Southern ports. To accomplish this, the U.S. Navy needed to capture Southern port cities that could supply a line of navy warships in coastal waters. The U.S. troops also needed to take control of the Mississippi River, which provided water access to and from the nation's interior.

The problem for the North was that the Southern coastline stretched for more than 3,000 miles (4,827 km), from Virginia to Texas, and included 189 harbors. The Union navy had only forty-two ships, and at least thirty of those were patrolling waters elsewhere.

Throughout 1861 and 1862, the Union navy bought or chartered numerous merchant ships. Once armed, these ships were sent off to join the blockade. Within nine months, the Union had placed 260 warships and commissioned the building of one hundred more. This period also saw the first of the ironclads, ships plated with thick iron, which would permanently change the way the United States waged war at sea.

With ironclads on both sides and Union ships outnumbering those of the Confederates, the Confederate navy could not hope to battle naval forces at sea successfully. Confederate leaders decided instead to attack Northern merchant ships, hoping to upset the Northern economy and draw U.S. warships away from the blockade to defend the merchant ships. The strategy did not work, although some damage was done to Northern shipping.

The Confederacy, meanwhile, urgently needed supplies from Europe. Some Southern ships concentrated on running, or breaking through, the blockade. Yet they could not keep up with the shipping needs of the South. Throughout the

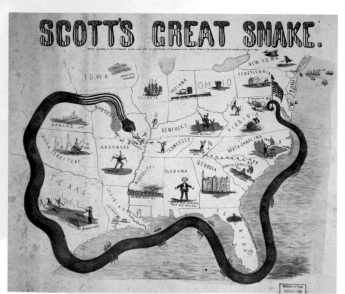

SCOTT'S GREAT SNAKE.

The Civil War

war, the Union blockade decreased the number of ships entering and leaving Southern ports by more than one-half.

The First Two Years

In the first two years of the Civil War, the greater number of victories went to the South. The Confederates won notable battles, for example, in Virginia at Bull Run (July 21, 1861, and August 29–30, 1862), Winchester (May 25, 1862), Cedar Mountain (August 9, 1862), and Fredericksburg (December 13, 1862). At the same time, the North made progress in western parts of the South. In Tennessee, on February 1862, Union general Ulysses S. Grant captured Fort Henry on the Tennessee River and Fort Donelson on the Cumberland River. These victories gave the North significant routes into the South's heartland.

On April 6–7, 1862, the two sides fought the Battle of Shiloh, in Tennessee. The North won, but at a terrible cost. Twenty thousand men lay dead or wounded by the end of the battle. One Tennessee private later recorded seeing "the dead…with their eyes wide open, the wounded begging piteously for help." General Sherman declared, "The scenes on this field would have cured anybody of war."

Even so, the war continued. On April 28, 1862, Admiral David G. Farragut led a Union fleet of eighteen warships and twenty smaller boats to break through Confederate defenses at the mouth of the Mississippi River. Farragut's forces took control of New Orleans, Louisiana, then continued upriver and captured Baton Rouge, Louisiana, and Natchez, Mississippi. Meanwhile, a fleet of Union ironclads steamed south on the river and captured Memphis, Tennessee. With that, only one city, Vicksburg, Mississippi, kept the Union from controlling the Mississippi River.

The Ironclads

When the Civil War began, the Confederacy had no navy and little shipbuilding capacity. In self-defense, the South pioneered a new kind of ship—the ironclad.

Southern shipbuilders used an abandoned wooden U.S. Navy ship, the *Merrimack*, for their first ironclad. They covered the ship's upper portions with thick iron plates, armed the ship, and mounted it with a long, heavy iron ram. They renamed the ship the *Virginia* and launched it on February 17, 1862.

On March 8, the *Virginia* encountered three Union ships off Hampton Roads, Virginia. The ironclad sank two ships and ran a third aground before retreating. The next day, the *Virginia*'s crew was surprised to find that the Union had sent its own ironclad, the *Monitor*, to match iron with iron. In the battle that followed, both ships proved their superiority to wooden warships. In the future, the United States would turn exclusively to iron ships for its navy.

CHAPTER 4

Emancipation

▼ A sketch published in 1892 shows an African American man (probably a former slave) begging President Lincoln to allow him to join the Union troops in fighting the Confederacy during the Civil War. African Americans were eventually allowed to join Union troops in 1862.

While the armies and navies of the North and South faced each other at gunpoint, Northern abolitionists, both black and white, launched a war of words that was not about politics or property. It was about the freedom of four million African Americans living in slavery. Nothing short of complete abolition—the end of slavery everywhere in the country and for all time—should be tolerated, they said.

From the beginning, President Lincoln had refused to make slavery the centerpiece of the war. He did not want to lose the support of the Border States, which had slavery but did not secede. He also wanted to leave the door open to the Confederate states to return to the Union without the financial

disaster that giving up their slaves would cause. He insisted before Congress, on July 4, 1861, that he had "no purpose, directly or indirectly, to interfere with slavery in the States where it exists."

No one, however, could prevent slavery from becoming a major issue during the war. As Union troops captured territory in the South, slaves were escaping in great numbers, taking shelter behind Union lines. Although Union officers at first returned the slaves to their masters, in accordance with the Fugitive Slave Act, they began to question the wisdom of this move.

One Union general, Benjamin F. Butler, refused to return fugitive slaves that he knew had helped build fortifications for the Confederates. These people, he said, were "**contrabands** of war," meaning that it was fair to keep them to prevent them from aiding the enemy. Other military leaders had great qualms of conscience about sending these desperate run-aways back into slavery, knowing that they would face terrible punishments.

What to Do With the Slaves?

One esteemed black abolitionist, Frederick Douglass, argued forcefully that the end of slavery was the only acceptable reason for the war. "Now is the time to put an end to all our present national calamities," he proclaimed. "Any attempt to secure peace to the whites while leaving the blacks in chains...will be labor lost.... The war now being waged in this land is a war for and against slavery." Other abolitionists followed his lead, speaking out at rallies, writing articles for newspapers, and sending petitions to the government.

At the same time, dismay grew among Northerners over the terrible bloodshed of the war.

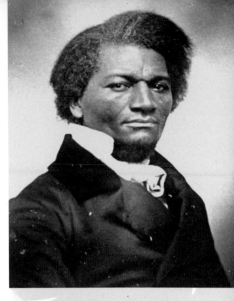

Frederick Douglass (1818–1895)

Frederick Douglass, pictured here, was born into slavery in Maryland in 1818. As a teenager, he was hired out to a violent **slave breaker** who treated him with terrible cruelty. Douglass described himself at that point as "broken in body, soul, and spirit."

In 1838, Douglass escaped to freedom in the North and became an abolitionist. When he spoke about his life under slavery at the Massachusetts Anti-Slavery Society, it was reported that "flinty hearts were pierced, and cold ones melted by his eloquence."

Douglass published his own antislavery newspaper, the *North Star*, and became a trusted adviser to Lincoln, helping to recruit Northern African Americans for the Union army.

United States Colored Troops

About 180,000 African Americans joined the Union military forces. Many others served without becoming soldiers, working as laborers supporting the U.S. troops.

The black regiments of the U.S. Colored Troops (USCT) fought in hundreds of battles. At first, even as enlisted men, the African Americans were given noncombat duty. Eventually, though, they were allowed to prove themselves in battle.

The men of the USCT distinguished themselves as soldiers. At least thirty-eight thousand African Americans died in the Civil War of disease or battle wounds. The U.S. government awarded the Congressional Medal of Honor to twenty-four black soldiers in recognition of gallant service.

Fewer men came forward to enlist, and families demanded that their husbands and sons be allowed to come home. African American men, however, were clamoring for the chance to fight in the war. They showed up at enlistment centers and were turned away. They sent petitions to the War Department and were turned down. They wanted the chance to prove they were as loyal to the Union as whites and as worthy of the rights of free citizens. Some white Northerners began to favor the idea of allowing African Americans to fight.

The pressure was now on Lincoln. His great aim remained the preservation of the Union, but he needed new leverage to keep Northern support and to push the South to surrender. In September 1862, he issued an early draft of what would become the Emancipation Proclamation. It stated that unless the Confederate states (the states that had seceded) put down their arms and returned to the Union by January 1, 1863, all the slaves in Confederate states, even those not occupied by the Union army, would be "then, henceforward, and forever free." The South did not bow to Lincoln's challenge, and on January 1, 1863, Lincoln signed a final version of the Emancipation Proclamation into law. In addition to legally freeing slaves in the Confederate states, the proclamation stated that all free African Americans would "be received into the armed service of the United States." Abolitionists and African Americans throughout the North celebrated news of the Proclamation's signing. In the South, little changed. Freedom on paper meant nothing to the slaves there until the Civil War ended. Even after the official end of the war in April 1865, the news spread slowly. In the outposts of Texas, slaves did not learn of the Emancipation Proclamation until June 19. That date gained the name "Juneteenth," marking the official celebration of freedom among black Americans.

Northern Victories

The North had enjoyed few significant victories and suffered many disastrous defeats into the first half of the war's third year. That was about to change, in large part because of the influx of tens of thousands of African American army and navy recruits.

In the spring of 1863, after much effort, General Ulysses Grant finally managed to surround Vicksburg, the last Confederate stronghold on the Mississippi River. After failing to storm the Southern defenses, he laid **siege** to the city, cutting off all outside sources of supply. The siege continued from May 22 until July 4, when the Confederate forces finally surrendered. As the Union soldiers entered the city, they shared their food with the starving enemy. One Vicksburg woman would later recall, "What a contrast [these] stalwart, well-fed men, so splendidly set-up and accoutered [were] to...the worn men in gray."

On the very day that Vicksburg fell to the Union, another major battle was won in the East, in Gettysburg, Pennsylvania. General Robert E. Lee, commander of the Confederate forces, was leading his army north, intending to attack Harrisburg, Pennsylvania. On the first of July, he arrived at the small town of Gettysburg, about 39 miles (62 km) south of Harrisburg. There he met Union forces under the command of General George Gordon Meade. For three days, the armies fought. By the time the smoke cleared on July 4, with Lee's army in retreat, Lee had lost one-third of his army (3,903 killed and 24,000 wounded or missing). The Union army was down by one-quarter (3,155 killed and 20,000 wounded or missing.)

The Gettysburg Address

On November 19, 1863, Lincoln delivered a short speech at the close of ceremonies dedicating the battlefield cemetery at Gettysburg:

Four score and seven years ago our fathers brought forth upon this continent a new nation, conceived in liberty, and dedicated to the proposition that all men are created equal.

Now we are engaged in a great civil war, testing whether that nation, or any nation so conceived and so dedicated, can long endure. We are met on a great battlefield of that war.

...It is for us the living... to be dedicated here to the unfinished work which they who fought here have thus far so nobly advanced. It is...for us to be here dedicated to the great task remaining before us, that from these honored dead we take increased devotion to that cause for which they gave the last full measure of devotion, that we here highly resolve that these dead shall not have died in vain—that this nation, under God, shall have a new birth of freedom—and that government of the people, by the people, for the people shall not perish from the earth.

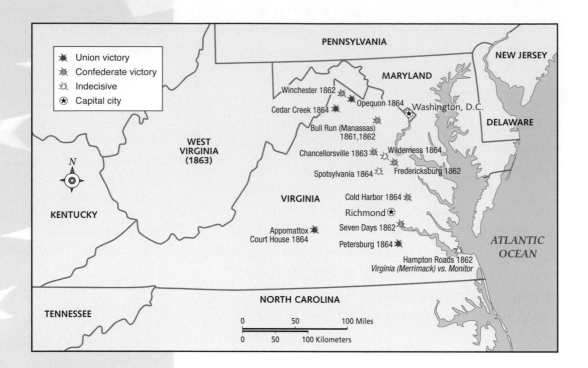

The legend reads:

- ✳ Union victory
- ✳ Confederate victory
- ✳ Indecisive
- ⊛ Capital city

PENNSYLVANIA

NEW JERSEY

MARYLAND

Winchester 1862

Opequon 1864

Washington, D.C.

Cedar Creek 1864

DELAWARE

Bull Run (Manassas) 1861, 1862

WEST VIRGINIA (1863)

Chancellorsville 1863

Wilderness 1864

Spotsylvania 1864

Fredericksburg 1862

KENTUCKY

VIRGINIA

Cold Harbor 1864

Richmond ⊛

Appomattox Court House 1864

Seven Days 1862

ATLANTIC OCEAN

Petersburg 1864

Hampton Roads 1862
Virginia (Merrimack) vs. Monitor

TENNESSEE

NORTH CAROLINA

0   50   100 Miles

0   50   100 Kilometers

▲ This map illustrates Civil War battles fought in Virginia, a state that saw more battles than any other. The site of the famous "Battle of the Ironclads" between the Union Monitor *and Confederate* Virginia *(formerly the* Merrimack*) at Hampton Roads on the coast is also noted.*

The Turning Point of the War

Although the war was far from over, many historians believe that the victories at Vicksburg and Gettysburg turned the war permanently in the North's favor. With Vicksburg captured, the Union finally had control of the Mississippi, cutting a major transportation and supply line for the South. Lee's defeat at Gettysburg so humiliated the general that he offered President Davis his resignation, which Davis refused.

The North went on to win several important battles in Tennessee in the fall of 1863. These victories left the Union forces well placed to cut across Georgia and capture Atlanta. Southerners began to fear that they could not win. As one Richmond inhabitant wrote, "gloom and unspoken despondency hang like a pall everywhere."

CHAPTER 5

Civilians in Time of War

The Civil War was not just about soldiers, guns, and political issues. It also drew civilians into the business and work of war. Some served behind the scenes with the army. Others joined the effort on the home front.

The longer the Civil War continued, the more involved ordinary civilians became. Hundreds of thousands of men went off to war, leaving the work of farms, factories, and mills to those they left behind. In large part, men too old to fight and women stepped in to fill the labor gap.

▼ *This 1865 photograph of Clara Barton, the founder of the American Red Cross, taken by renowned Civil War photographer Matthew Brady, is the most famous and widely circulated photograph of the famous humanitarian.*

Civilians at Home and at War

During the Civil War, the huge number of men who left homes and businesses to become soldiers led to innovations that could replace their labor. On farms in the North, women who could afford it bought recently improved types of machines, such as threshers and reapers, to help accomplish the work their husbands had typically done. One observer

29

Clara Barton (1821–1912)

"Women don't know anything about war," Clara Barton once said. "I wish men didn't either. They have always known a great deal too much about it for the good of their kind."

Once the Civil War began, Barton resigned from the Patent Office to work as a volunteer delivering supplies to the front lines of the war. She organized a relief program for soldiers and an organization to distribute donated medical supplies to battlefields. Before long, U.S. surgeon general William A. Hammond gave her permission to go onto the battlefields herself "for the purpose of distributing comforts for the sick and wounded, and nursing them." Barton became known as the "Angel of the Battlefield." She went on to organize a program to locate men missing in action. After the war's end, Barton founded the American Red Cross, which continues the work of disaster relief today.

noted: "So perfect is machinery, that men seem to be of less necessity.... A stout matron whose sons are in the army...cut seven acres [of hay] with ease in a day, riding leisurely upon her cutter." In the North, food production remained high during the war, actually increasing to the point that wheat, corn, pork, and beef could be exported to Europe.

In both the North and South, many women (and, in the South, slaves) went to work at factories where supplies for the war were made. Guns, ammunition, wagons, boots, and clothing were in constant demand. Other businesses had to be kept going, as well, and nonfighters stepped in and did jobs that soldiers had formerly done, such as working in textile factories.

Women on both sides of the conflict also made their way to the war zones and army camps. Women often traveled with soldier husbands, bringing children along. In the camps, they cooked, sewed, and did laundry. "Soldiers' wives and sisters who had come to see their friends and stayed," according to one observer, acted as nurses on the battlefield. Some women did exactly the work that a doctor would do. Most often they served in makeshift army hospitals. Some were paid; others volunteered.

Battlefield Industries

Some workers had businesses they were able to carry to the battlefield. The Civil War drew numbers of photographers, artists, and journalists to the battle zones, all hoping to capture the action and record the facts for the people at home. Many of these on-the-scene people used their depictions of war to promote their personal political views. Some artists, for example, depicted battles with cleaned-up, glory-filled images of war heroes and great victories (with the victory going to their own side of the conflict).

The Civil War

Even photographers could play with the facts. Many historians believe that some of the images of dead soldiers on the battlefield were staged. The soldiers were certainly dead, but their bodies might be placed in a position that looked dramatic or implied action that had not really happened. Even so, photographic images of war could not be changed enough to make it look glamorous.

With tens of thousands of men dying in battle, a great need arose for embalmers and coffin makers, who would set up their businesses near a battle scene, since the armies were not able to send bodies home for burial. Although some bodies were left where they fell, laborers were usually sent out to gather the dead and bring them to camp so the bodies could be buried. In the Confederate army, this job often fell to African American slaves. For Northern troops, black noncombatants attached to a regiment would be given the job.

African Americans in the South

Some Southern slaveholders moved their slaves inland away from the invading Union army forces. Still hoping to win the war, these Southerners wanted to protect their slave "property." Some African Americans, both slave and free, were put to work by the Confederate army, building fortifications and laboring in other ways such as cooking and laundering to support the soldiers of the South. Slaves who were kept on Southern **plantations** were expected to continue the farmwork in order to make sure there would be food for the army. Yet many slaves, although they did not rebel, slowed or stopped their work. Some Southern women complained that the attitudes of their black servants had become disrespectful.

Harriet Tubman (1820?–1913)

Harriet Tubman, pictured here, was born into slavery in Maryland. In 1849, she fled to freedom in Philadelphia, Pennsylvania, with the help of the Underground Railroad, a secret network of people who sneaked escaped slaves to freedom.

In Philadelphia, Tubman became an abolitionist. After the passage of the Fugitive Slave Act, when it became illegal to help a runaway slave, she joined the Underground Railroad and led more than three hundred slaves to free states or to Canada.

During the war, Tubman worked in the South as a nurse, a scout, and a spy for the Union army. Called "Moses" (after the biblical Moses who led the Israelites to freedom), she became such a legend that Southerners offered $40,000 in rewards for her capture. The money was never collected.

▲ In an undated photograph taken by renowned Civil War photographer Matthew Brady during the Civil War, an African American soldier (and former slave) with the rank of mess corporal (a field cook) serves officers at the federal headquarters of the Union army in Belle Plain, Virginia.

During and after the war, some slaves who had been left behind by evacuating slaveholders moved onto deserted property and set up their own small holdings. The Freedmen's Bureau was established by Congress to supervise all relief and educational activities related to former slaves, including issuing rations, clothes, and medicine. The bureau helped slaves rent or buy the property they occupied. Most slaves tried to escape in the confusion of war. Behind Union lines, thousands of slaves lived in "contraband camps." The conditions were often poor, and many slaves arrived with only the clothes on their backs and a few meager possessions. Some went farther north, often traveling the secret network of the Underground Railroad, hoping finally to escape the chains of slavery. One and all wanted one thing, and that was freedom.

War and Religion

Religious leaders played their own important parts in the Civil War. Early in the war, some of them put aside their usual prohibitions about mixing preaching and politics. As they became caught up in the conflict like other civilians, they chose sides and argued that God, too, was on their favored side of the war.

The Civil War

In the South, many ministers defended slavery, claiming it was supported in the Bible, and preached the holiness of defending against an attacking enemy. In the North, many ministers joined ranks with the abolitionists and preached about a righteous war that would set enslaved people free.

Black ministers in the North and the South preached freedom to their black congregations. They compared the plight of the enslaved African Americans to that of the Israelites enslaved in ancient Egypt. Just as God had set the Israelites free and defeated Egypt's army, so would God set the slaves of the South free and defeat the Confederate army. Such words gave blacks throughout the nation courage to fight for freedom against terrible odds.

Ministers had their place among the fighting men as well. Armies employed chaplains to preach on Sundays, lead soldiers in prayer before they went into battle, and generally encourage the troops to believe that God was on their side. Black regiments employed African American ministers who urged the troops on with assurances that their cause was righteous. Many of the soldiers—black and white, Union and Confederate—were hardly more than boys. They were lonely, frightened, and longing for their faraway homes and families. For many of them, the chaplains provided comfort and a sense of safety.

It was not only African Americans and fighting soldiers who turned to religion for comfort and some understanding of what was happening. The war claimed more than half a million lives and ended the enslavement of four million people. For all the people who were living through the conflict, the world had been upended, and many turned to religion for stability and consolation.

From Drummer to General

The Civil War drew everyone into its turmoil, including children. In 1861, nine-year-old John Lincoln Clem, (1851–1937), pictured here, ran away from his home in Newark, Ohio, to join the Union army. When told that the army "wasn't enlisting infants," he tagged along as a drummer boy. Officers of the regiment rewarded his determination by pitching in donations to pay him a soldier's salary of $13 a month.

In April 1862, Johnny Clem's regiment took part in the battle at Shiloh. Clem's drum was shattered by artillery fire, earning him the nickname "Johnny Shiloh." In 1863, at the Battle of Chickamauga in Georgia, he shot a Confederate officer and became known nationally as the "Drummer Boy of Chickamauga."

Clem remained in the army for the rest of his working days. By the time he retired in 1916, he had earned the rank of major general.

CHAPTER 6

The Fight to End the War

In the final year of the Civil War, the horrors of war were felt in the United States as never before. Tens of thousands of men who were captured on the battlefield were sent to deadly prisoner-of-war camps. In battlefield areas of the South, civilians lost their homes and livelihood. Even as the time neared when emancipation would become a reality, racial **prejudice** continued and even increased in all the states.

In March 1864, Ulysses S. Grant, who had become general-in-chief of all the Union armies and personally commanded the Army of the Potomac (the Union army's largest division), prepared to fight Robert E. Lee and his Army of Northern Virginia (the Confederate Army's largest division) to the finish. Grant intended to battle his way past defensive Confederate troops to the Confederate capital, Richmond.

▼ *Florence Military Stockade, a Confederate prisoner-of-war camp in Florence, South Carolina, held between fifteen thousand and eighteen thousand Union soldiers from September 1864 to February 1865. This watercolor painted by James E. Taylor in 1897 is titled* Counting Us Off *and illustrates prisoners being counted by guards as they walk across a bridge on the grounds of the prison camp.*

The two opposing armies fought battle after battle in Virginia, first in the Wilderness (May 6), then in Spotsylvania (May 12) and in Cold Harbor (June 1). Sixty thousand Union soldiers died and roughly half that many Confederates. Still, Grant had not reached Richmond, so he settled down to a long siege of Petersburg, the rail center south of Richmond that connected the capital to the rest of the Confederacy.

The Death Pens

Meanwhile, soldiers who had been taken prisoner in the war suffered their own agonies in the prison camps. More than 150 prisons were set up during the war, in forts, existing jails, army barracks, and tent cities surrounded by tall fences. Every one of these prison camps ended up filled beyond capacity.

Historians estimate that at least fifty-six thousand men died in Civil War prisons. Neither the North nor the South intended these deaths. Both sides endured extreme shortages of shelter, food, and clothing. The prisoners suffered malnutrition. Their wounds became infected and turned to gangrene. The result was a death rate that surpassed that of any battle fought in the war.

The worst and most notorious prison of the war was the Confederate-run prison in Andersonville, Georgia. There, out of the almost thirty-three thousand prisoners of war it housed at its fullest, thirteen thousand died.

Political Pressures

While the war dragged on in the summer and fall of 1864, Lincoln faced another presidential election. He faced outraged criticism about the prison camps and Northern objections to his plans for the South after the

"Bummers"

In 1864, Union general William Tecumseh Sherman marched his army through the South, from Atlanta to Savannah, Georgia, effectively destroying the region and ending the Civil War.

While Sherman and his army cut a path through the heart of the Confederacy, a large group of foragers, who raided farms and homes in towns along the march, followed along after the army. Some of the foragers were deserters or soldiers who were absent without leave. Others simply had nowhere else to be.

These men came to be known as "bummers." Spreading out over the countryside in the wake of the army, the bummers simply robbed and destroyed any civilian property left behind by Sherman's men. Although Sherman knew of the bummers' activities, there is no evidence that he ever tried to stop them. Some historians believe that Sherman, wanting to punish the South, let the bummers run wild as a way of accomplishing what he could not "officially" do with his commissioned soldiers.

▲ In preparation for his "March to the Sea," General William T. Sherman inspects his troops and artillery before setting out for Atlanta in 1864.

war. His program of **Reconstruction** seemed far too easygoing to many Northerners. They wanted to punish the South. Lincoln wanted to build a united future that the South could accept.

Lincoln's chances for the coming election received a boost with the news of the capture of Atlanta by Union general William Tecumseh Sherman on September 1, 1864. Lincoln won the election with 55 percent of the popular vote.

Meanwhile, Sherman decided to use his invasion of Georgia to convince the Southern civilian population to give up. Setting out from Atlanta on November 16, Sherman's troops traveled through Georgia to Milledgeville, then the capital of the state, and reached Savannah on December 21, 1864. On the way, they destroyed everything in their path in what later came to be called Sherman's "March to the Sea." Sherman wrote, "those who brought war into our country deserve all the curses and maledictions a people can pour out." Grant backed him up with orders to "create havoc and destruction of all resources that would be beneficial to the enemy."

The Final Campaign

The Civil War ended in Virginia. At Petersburg in March 1865, Lee's weary army tried to break through Union lines to end the siege that had begun months earlier. Grant had new reinforcements, however, and Lee's army was driven back. On April 9, 1865, Lee's army surrendered. The fighting at

The Civil War

Petersburg had cost the Union army 10,780 men. Six thousand Confederate soldiers had died, and another 27,800 were captured.

At a house near the village of Appomattox Court House, Lee and Grant faced each other across a table. Grant offered generous terms. The two sides would no longer be enemies, after all, but fellow citizens of the United States. "The Confederates were now our prisoners," Grant later said, "and we did not want to exult over their downfall." He decided that the Confederate prisoners would be paroled instead of sentenced to time in prison. They would be allowed to keep personal property, including their horses, and provided with food. Grant prohibited his own Union soldiers from celebrating the surrender.

At the formal surrender on April 9, the Confederate soldiers laid down their arms, stacking their weapons and ammunition before a line of Union soldiers. One Northern soldier later recalled a Southerner commenting as he laid his gun down, "Good-bye gun; I am darned glad to get rid of you."

From Joy to Sorrow

While the white South wept, Northerners and African Americans rejoiced at victory. Less than a week later, however, came the news that the North's president, Abraham Lincoln, had been assassinated. On April 14, Lincoln and his wife, Mary, attended a play at Ford's Theater, in Washington, D.C. There, an ardent pro-Confederate actor named John Wilkes Booth shot the president in the head.

Lincoln's death came at the end of the deadliest war in U.S. history. About 620,000 soldiers had died. Another 500,000 were wounded, 75,000 of whom would die of their wounds. An estimated 50,000 Southern civilians died as a direct result of the war.

Laying Lincoln to Rest

"On the Avenue in front of the White House were several hundred colored people, mostly women and children, weeping and wailing their loss," wrote Secretary of the Navy Gideon Welles on the morning after Lincoln's assassination. "This crowd did not diminish through the whole of that cold, wet day."

Thousands more mourners filed past Lincoln's casket as it lay on display in the White House East Room. Then the casket was taken by funeral train to Lincoln's hometown, Springfield, Illinois, for burial.

The train took two weeks to travel 1,662 miles (2,674 km). In Philadelphia, a double line of mourners stretched for 3 miles (4.8 km). In New York City, the casket rested in City Hall while the procession of mourners continued for four hours. In Cleveland, the casket was set up in an outdoor pavilion and visited by ten thousand mourners. A final stop was made at the County Courthouse in Chicago. Then the train carried Lincoln's coffin to its final destination, where thousands of mourners watched as it was placed in its vault.

CHAPTER 7

National Reunion

After four years, the Civil War was over. Dead, as well, were the notion of secession and the practice of slavery. The day of "these United States" had ended, along with the division of the country between "slave" and "free." In the future, Americans would come to speak of the United States as one nation, with a central government that placed important restrictions on the state governments. The expansion of federal power would show itself quickly in the Thirteenth, Fourteenth, and Fifteenth **Amendments** to the U.S. Constitution.

Abolitionists had won their long-fought battle to end slavery. Now it remained to work out what freedom would mean for four million newly emancipated slaves, as well as the free blacks, who also would have the rights of citizenship for the first time. Although laws could be passed that made equal rights the legal reality in the United States, laws could not control the way people felt. As the period of Reconstruction and its aftermath all too clearly showed, centuries of slavery and racial prejudice could not easily be erased.

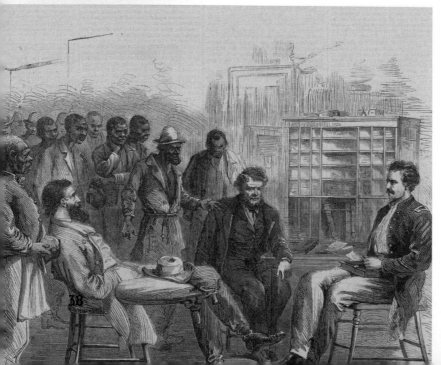

▼ African Americans, eager to be heard, crowd behind officials of the Freedmen's Bureau in Memphis, Tennessee. Intermittent rioting due to simmering racial tension between blacks and local white police officers began on the evening of April 30, 1866, in Memphis and ended four days later.

A National Conscience

With the death of Abraham Lincoln, his vice president, Andrew Johnson, took the presidential office. A former slaveholder and Southern Democrat, he had the job of carrying out the vision of the Republican president who had written the Emancipation Proclamation.

Johnson began his presidency with proclamations that granted pardons to anyone taking an oath of loyalty to the Union and supporting emancipation. He excluded former Confederate officials and large property owners, unless they applied individually to the president for the pardon.

Next Johnson appointed short-term governors for the former Confederate states and instructed them to call constitutional conventions (whose delegates were to be chosen by white voters with pardons). If the states ratified a new state **constitution** abolishing slavery, nullified acts of secession, and forgave all Confederate debts, they could reenter the Union.

Southern state governments immediately passed laws, which became known as Black Codes, severely restricting the rights of freedmen (slaves who had been freed) in ways that did not apply to any white person. The codes prevented free blacks from owning firearms and controlled where they could rent property, what public places they could frequent, and what kinds of contracts they could make.

Impeachment

As Reconstruction progressed, it became clear that President Johnson was at odds with those members of Congress who supported equal rights for the newly freed African Americans. While Congress acted to protect the civil rights of African Americans

The Thirteenth Amendment

In the Thirteenth Amendment, the United States recognized the equal rights of every human being in the country. The amendment states, "Neither slavery nor involuntary servitude, except as a punishment for crime whereof the party shall have been duly convicted, shall exist within the United States, or any place subject to their jurisdiction."

At last, the cause of African American freedom was firmly tied to the bedrock laws of the United States. The U.S. Senate passed the amendment by more than the required two-thirds approval. On January 31, 1865, the amendment passed in the House of Representatives, although by a narrow margin. Onlookers and members of Congress alike erupted in an outburst of noise and celebration. Then Congress took the rest of the day off "in honor of this immortal and sublime event."

It would take nearly another year before the needed three-quarters of the states had ratified the Thirteenth Amendment. On December 18, 1865, the Constitution finally declared legal slavery a thing of the past.

The Freedmen's Bureau

In March 1865, Congress created the Bureau of Refugees, Freedmen, and Abandoned Lands (commonly called the Freedmen's Bureau) to look after the welfare of ex-slaves. Slavery had created miseries that would take a long time to repair. Most of the freed people were left in extremely poor circumstances. The bureau provided food, clothing, and medical care. It divided abandoned or confiscated property and rented it in 40-acre (16-hectare) lots to former slaves.

Bureau workers also connected freed people with Northern relief societies, which raised funds to buy land, build schools and churches, pay teachers' salaries, and provide books and furniture for schools. Freed people wanted jobs so they could provide for themselves, yet they were often unfairly treated by former slaveholders. Bureau agents were sometimes called in to settle disputes or write a fair labor contract. Agents for the Freedmen's Bureau also helped reunite family members who had been sold by slave owners or lost in the confusion of the Civil War.

in the post-emancipation South, Johnson did all he could to undo its work. Johnson opposed equal-rights for blacks mainly on political grounds: he wanted the votes of Southern Democrats in the next presidential election. He also, however, quietly opposed equal rights because of his own personal prejudice. He did not believe that black people were the equals of white people. He thought that giving blacks equal rights would not be good for them or the country.

Congress divided the secessionist states into districts and placed military regiments in charge of enforcing Reconstruction laws. In response, Johnson replaced military leaders with men who sympathized more with the South than did the Northern Republicans who, at the time, were the dominant members of Congress. The fight between Johnson and Congress peaked when Johnson tried to remove Secretary of War Edwin Stanton from his post. Stanton was the critical link between Congress and the Union army in the South. The Republicans argued that Stanton's term of office was not over, which made Johnson's act illegal.

The Republican Congress took Johnson to court in a process called impeachment. The Constitution allows impeachment for "treason, bribery, or other high crimes and misdemeanors." The Senate charged the president with crimes against the government. If the Senate won its case, Johnson would be removed from office. The trial lasted from March 13 to May 26, 1868. The Senate lost by one vote, and Johnson remained in office.

The Fourteenth and Fifteenth Amendments

Even before trying to remove Johnson from office, Congress began the process of providing equal rights

The Civil War

for African Americans by passing two constitutional amendments. The Fourteenth Amendment stated, "All persons born or naturalized [given U.S. citizen status after immigration] in the United States, and subject to the jurisdiction thereof, are citizens of the United States and of the State wherein they reside." This meant that any American, regardless of color, was a citizen with a citizen's rights. The amendment also said that no state could deny a citizen's rights "without due process of law."

The Fourteenth Amendment also guaranteed payment of Union war debts and denied national responsibility for debts or losses incurred by the Confederacy. Anyone who, as a public official, had taken an oath to support the Constitution and then supported the Confederacy lost the right to public office. Johnson vetoed the Fourteenth Amendment, but Congress passed it over his veto on July 9, 1868.

The year 1868 was a presidential election year. Republicans had failed to remove Andrew Johnson from office through impeachment. Now they hoped to replace him through the election. They nominated the popular Union war hero Ulysses S. Grant. Grant wanted to make peace with the South. At the same time, he supported the Reconstruction aims of Congress. By a close popular vote but a huge Electoral College majority, Grant replaced Johnson as president.

In the aftermath of the election, Congress wrote the Fifteenth Amendment

▼ *This poster celebrating the Fifteenth Amendment was published in 1870. The center illustration of a parade is surrounded by small portraits and depictions of African American life. A list of the titles of different pictures, including* Reading the Emancipation Proclamation, Education Will Prove the Equality [of] the Races, The Ballot Box Is Open to Use, *and* We Till Our Own Fields, *is listed at the bottom of the print.*

to the Constitution. Blacks had not been permitted to vote in eleven Northern states and all the Border States. The Fifteenth Amendment, ratified on February 3, 1870, guaranteed all adult male citizens the right to vote, no matter what their "race, color, or previous condition of servitude." (The amendment did not apply to female citizens because they did not have voting privileges at the time.) It also gave Congress the power to enforce this right at a state level.

Reconstruction

Reconstruction sought to wipe out the racial abuses of slavery. It encouraged new Southern state constitutions that ensured black rights; it passed amendments to the U.S. Constitution; and it gave practical help in the form of land, education, and money for newly freed people. On the other hand, Southern state governments did everything short of returning to a slave society to keep African Americans in an inferior position. Southern states insisted on racially separate schools and churches. They created local laws, called "Jim Crow" laws, which originated as the Black Codes but soon went further. The laws segregated seats on public transportation and in restaurants and barred African Americans from public places such as pools, parks, and hospitals.

As prejudiced Southern whites rebuilt their lives, some of them stoked their hatreds as well. One of the most violent times in U.S. history ensued, as white racists "punished" blacks for trying to vote, for refusing to step aside on a path, or for simply looking directly at a white person. A vicious terrorist organization, the Ku Klux Klan, assaulted and murdered blacks and sympathetic whites.

Some progress would be made, but it would be slow and tortuous. Although the U.S. government emerged

President Lincoln hoped that the Freedman's Bureau would adopt his goal of providing land for newly freed African Americans. His plan, oficially called Special Field Orders, no. 15, was issued by General William T. Sherman and became known as "40 acres and a mule." General Sherman gave freedmen the land owned by their previous masters in regions along the coasts of South Carolina, Georgia, and Florida. However, in 1825 President Johnson returned the land to its previous owners.

The Civil War

much stronger in the aftermath of the Civil War, its provisions for racial equality could not fix the centuries of damage done by racial prejudice and slavery.

Contradicting the ideals that the country was founded on, ongoing racial inequality would haunt the nation into the next century, when civil rights movements would seek once again to right wrongs.

▲ *Homeless black men are rounded up by police in New Orleans in 1864 in accordance with the Black Codes that restricted the liberty of African Americans.*

The Civil War transformed the United States. During the fighting, technological innovations multiplied as miles of railroad tracks and telegraph lines were laid and as farms and factories used mechanical devices to replace the many men who had gone to war. Many former slaves moved into Northern urban areas looking for new opportunities, education, and better way of life. People left homes and property destroyed in the war and moved west, where new territories and states offered new chances for prosperity.

The Civil War, meanwhile, continues to produce endless conversations, articles, books, movies, and documentaries. It continues to preoccupy the imaginations of citizens nationwide, as do the issues of civil liberties, state versus federal power, and equal rights that led the nation to war in the first place. The country continues to struggle with educational, economic, and racial inequalities that laws have so far failed to heal. The United States is now one nation. Whether it will ever fully heal the wounds created by slavery and the most destructive war in American history is yet to be decided.

TIME LINE

1850	Congress completes the passage of the Compromise of 1850.
1852	Harriet Beecher Stowe publishes the abolitionist novel *Uncle Tom's Cabin*.
1854	Congress passes the Kansas-Nebraska Act.
1856	John Brown leads a raid in Pottawatomie, Kansas, that results in the kidnapping and murder of five proslavery citizens. Brown would be executed in 1859.
1857	The U.S. Supreme Court denies Dred Scott's appeal for his freedom from slavery.
1858	Abraham Lincoln and Stephen A. Douglas face each other in seven debates before the election for U.S. senator from Illinois.
1860	Abraham Lincoln wins the presidential election; South Carolina secedes from the Union.
1861	Mississippi, Florida, Alabama, Georgia, Louisiana, Texas, Virginia, Arkansas, North Carolina, and Tennessee secede from the Union; Lincoln is inaugurated as the sixteenth president of the United States; the Civil War begins with the fighting at Fort Sumter; Lincoln proclaims a blockade against Southern ports; Confederate forces win the First Battle of Bull Run in Virginia.
1862	Union general Ulysses S. Grant captures Fort Henry and Fort Donelson and secures important river routes into the South; Confederate forces launch their first ironclad warship, the CSS *Virginia*; Northern forces win the Battle of Shiloh in Tennessee; the Union navy under Admiral David G. Farragut breaks through Confederate forces at the mouth of the Mississippi River; Confederate forces win the Battles of Winchester, Cedar Mountain, and Fredericksburg, in Virginia.
1863	Lincoln signs the Emancipation Proclamation; Vicksburg falls to Union forces; Confederate forces surrender control of the Mississippi River to Grant; Union forces under General George Gordon Meade defeat Confederate troops under General Robert E. Lee at Gettysburg; Lincoln delivers the Gettysburg Address.
1864	Grant becomes general-in-chief of the Union armies; General William Tecumseh Sherman captures Atlanta and begins his "March to the Sea."
1865	Congress passes the Thirteenth Amendment; the Thirteenth Amendment is ratified by December 18; Congress creates the Freedmen's Bureau; Lee surrenders the Confederate army to Grant; Lincoln is assassinated at Ford's Theater in Washington, D. C.; slaves in Texas become the last to learn of emancipation.
1868	President Andrew Johnson is impeached; Congress ratifies the Fourteenth Amendment despite Johnson's veto.
1870	Congress ratifies the Fifteenth Amendment.

GLOSSARY

abolition the legal end of slavery

amendments changes or additions to the U.S. Constitution

armaments the military forces and war equipment of a country

arsenal government facility for manufacturing and storing war material

assassinate to murder by surprise attack for political reasons

ballot a sheet of paper used for secret voting in an election

blockade use of troops or warships to prevent the passage of people or supplies to an enemy stronghold

citizen a person who has allegiance to a government and is entitled to protection from it

compromise an agreement that seeks to settle differences between two people or groups by each giving up something

constitution a document that establishes the powers and duties of a government and the rights and privileges of its citizens

contrabands escaped slaves during the Civil War who were taken behind Union lines

debate formal discussion of a topic by people holding opposing views

fleet a group of warships under a single command

"free-soil" term applied to people, states, or territories opposed to slavery

fugitive term applied to a person who escapes or flees

homesteading occupying and settling a place in order to claim ownership

inauguration a formal ceremony to mark the beginning of a term of office

indigo a plant that yields a commercially valuable, deep reddish-blue dye

militia a group of citizens organized for armed service in emergencies

pig iron a crude by-product of iron produced in a blast furnace; it may be used for armaments

plantations large farms planted with crops and worked by laborers who live there

prejudice hatred of a particular group, race, or religion

Reconstruction the reorganization of seceded states after the Civil War

representatives delegates who have the job of acting, voting, or deciding for another person or group of people

secession the act of formally withdrawing from an organization, as when a state withdraws from its nation

siege a blockade intended to force surrender

slave breaker a person given the job of teaching a slave to obey, often with the use of force and violence

telegraph a system of communication over a distance using a code sent in the form of electrical impulses

territories geographical areas under the partial or complete control of a government

FOR FURTHER INFORMATION

Books

DeFord, Deborah. *Joining the Union Forces: African Americans During the Civil War.* Facts On File, 2006.

Hunt, Irene. *Across Five Aprils.* Berkley, 1986.

King, David C. *Civil War and Reconstruction* (American Heritage, American Voices). Jossey-Bass, 2003.

Marrin, Albert. *Commander in Chief: Abraham Lincoln and the Civil War.* Dutton Children's Books, 2003.

Massie, Elizabeth. *1863: A House Divided: A Novel of the Civil War.* Tor Books, 2000.

McPherson, James. *Fields of Fury: The American Civil War.* Atheneum, 2002.

Reit, Seymour. *Behind Enemy Lines: The Incredible Story of Emma Edmonds, Civil War Spy.* Gulliver Books Paperbacks, 2001.

Web Sites

Africans in America, Part 4: Narrative: The Civil War
www.pbs.org/wgbh/aia/part4/4narr5.html

American Civil War
americancivilwar.com/

American Experience: Reconstruction: The Second Civil War
www.pbs.org/wgbh/amex/reconstruction/

The Civil War Through a Child's Eye
memory.loc.gov/learn/lessons/99/civilwar/resourc.html

Selected Civil War Photographs Home Page
memory.loc.gov/ammem/cwphtml/cwphome.html

Publisher's note to educators and parents: Our editors have carefully reviewed this Web site to ensure that it is suitable for children. Many Web sites change frequently, however, and we cannot guarantee that a site's future contents will continue to meet our high standards of quality and educational value. Be advised that children should be closely supervised whenever they access the Internet.

INDEX

About the Author

Deborah DeFord has written many books about the past and its influence on the way we live today. Her first fictional book for young people, *An Enemy Among Them*, told the story of one colonial family's experiences during the American Revolution. As a writer and editor for the children's magazine *U*S*Kids*, she authored numerous articles about nature, science, and the way things work. DeFord is also the author of *Wars That Changed American History: The American Revolution*. She resides in Connecticut.